THIS NOTEBOOK
BELONGS TO

NOTEBOOK

NOTEBOOK

NOTEBOOK

NOTEBOOK

NOTEBOOK

NOTEBOOK

NOTEBOOK

NOTEBOOK

NOTEBOOK

NOTEBOOK

NOTEBOOK

NOTEBOOK

NOTEBOOK

NOTEBOOK

NOTEBOOK

NOTEBOOK

NOTEBOOK

NOTEBOOK

NOTEBOOK

NOTEBOOK

NOTEBOOK

NOTEBOOK

NOTEBOOK

NOTEBOOK

NOTEBOOK

NOTEBOOK

NOTEBOOK

NOTEBOOK

NOTEBOOK

NOTEBOOK

NOTEBOOK

NOTEBOOK

NOTEBOOK

NOTEBOOK

NOTEBOOK

NOTEBOOK

NOTEBOOK

NOTEBOOK

NOTEBOOK

NOTEBOOK

NOTEBOOK

NOTEBOOK

NOTEBOOK

NOTEBOOK

NOTEBOOK

NOTEBOOK

NOTEBOOK

NOTEBOOK

NOTEBOOK

NOTEBOOK

NOTEBOOK

NOTEBOOK

NOTEBOOK

NOTEBOOK

NOTEBOOK

NOTEBOOK

NOTEBOOK

NOTEBOOK

NOTEBOOK

NOTEBOOK

NOTEBOOK

NOTEBOOK

NOTEBOOK

NOTEBOOK

NOTEBOOK

NOTEBOOK

NOTEBOOK

NOTEBOOK

NOTEBOOK

NOTEBOOK

NOTEBOOK

NOTEBOOK

NOTEBOOK

NOTEBOOK

NOTEBOOK

NOTEBOOK

NOTEBOOK

NOTEBOOK

NOTEBOOK

NOTEBOOK

NOTEBOOK

NOTEBOOK

NOTEBOOK

NOTEBOOK

NOTEBOOK

NOTEBOOK

NOTEBOOK

NOTEBOOK

NOTEBOOK

NOTEBOOK

NOTEBOOK

www.ingramcontent.com/pod-product-compliance
Lightning Source LLC
Chambersburg PA
CBHW070432220526
45466CB00004B/1641
* 9 7 8 1 6 7 8 3 4 2 8 0 7 *